# AFTER HASTINGS

Merryn Williams

# PREVIOUS BOOKS BY MERRYN WILLIAMS

*Poetry*
*The Sun's Yellow Eye*
*The Latin Master's Story*
*The First Wife's Tale*
*Letter to my Rival*
*The Fragile Bridge: New and Selected Poems*
*In the Spirit of Wilfred Owen* (ed.)
*The Georgians 1901–1930* (ed.)
*Poems for Jeremy Corbyn* (ed.)
*Strike up the Band: Poems for John Lucas at 80* (ed.)
*Poems for the Year 2020: Eighty Poets on the Pandemic* (ed.)
*Federico Garcia Lorca: Selected Poems* (translated)

*Prose*
*Preface to Hardy*
*Women in the English Novel 1800–1900*
*Margaret Oliphant: A Critical Biography*
*Six Women Novelists*
*Wilfred Owen*
*Clare and Effie* (for children)
*The Chalet Girls Grow Up*
*The Watsons* (Jane Austen's novel completed)
*Effie: A Victorian Scandal, From Ruskin's wife to Millais' Muse*
*Mansfield Park Revisited*

# AFTER HASTINGS

## MERRYN WILLIAMS

Shoestring Press

Printed by imprintdigital
Upton Pyne, Exeter
www.digital.imprint.co.uk

Typesetting and cover design by The Book Typesetters
hello@thebooktypesetters.com
07422 598 168
www.thebooktypesetters.com

Published by Shoestring Press
19 Devonshire Avenue, Beeston, Nottingham, NG9 1BS
(0115) 925 1827
www.shoestringpress.co.uk

First published 2023
© Copyright: Merryn Williams

The moral right of the author has been asserted.

ISBN 978-1-915553-24-9

# ACKNOWLEDGEMENTS

Poems have appeared in *Acumen*, *Anthroposphere*, *Artemis*, *Friends of the Dymock Poets Journal*, *The Frogmore Papers*, *The High Window*, *The Journal*, *London Grip*, *The Morning Star*, *Obsessed with Pipework*, *The Oxford Magazine*, *The Seventh Quarry*, *South Bank Poetry*, *The Wilfred Owen Association Journal*. 'Corona Days' appeared in **Corona Verses**, the first of the Covid anthologies, edited by Janine Booth.

in memory of Ruth Bidgood

# CONTENTS

# WILFRED OWEN REFLECTS

The moon is red.
Occasionally, in dreams,
I stand on a hill on the wrong side of the border,
gaze down into a neutral country, Spain.
If I'd had more sense,
I might have walked through that pass, under cover of
darkness,
and not come back again.

I could have gone
quite easily, soon have picked up another tongue,
sat in shirt-sleeves
reading the English papers
for war news, occasionally finding some old friend's name.

What would my children have said?
Perhaps I'd not have had them.
Perhaps, twenty years on
they'd have agreed that I did the intelligent thing.
Possibly younger men
will burn their call-up papers, run
in all directions, do
what I should have done – and of course, I would not be dead.

Now, as I most reluctantly
head for the front, whenever a shell screams,
'Haven't you got the wits to keep out of this?'
I think of that blotched moon.
But I am of my time.
Shouldering the burden of this generation,
I see my name
carved on white stone, high in the heart of London.

1

# THAT AUTUMN

everywhere trees broke out in topaz, crimson,
flame; a huge moon rose over the ancient buildings.
And I thought I'd got over it, but I had not.

The colour scale stretched from snowberry to privet;
bryony, rosehip, spindle ran riot in the hedgerows,
rare shades of purple, too; meanwhile, the red candles
of Lords and Ladies lit my dark passage home.

But I was back in a certain intensive care unit
whose doors had closed; I no longer had any reason
to go there.  Unripe crab apples strewed the towpath
that autumn, and sloe berries set my teeth on edge.

# THE CHILD'S TESTIMONY

I was with my father at a banquet
when the news came through that he had died.
Men in evening suits sprang up, ecstatic,
clapped and roared (while out there, people cried).

I was eight, knew nothing, but years later
heard my father saying to his wife
(unaware of me), 'Thank God it happened.
He would have destroyed our way of life'.

Now he's part of history; there are statues;
pious, double-tongued, the textbooks say
sugared things about his high achievement.
I am old.  I don't forget that day.

# LOOKING AT THE SNOW

I saw my neighbour looking at the snow
which started thickly falling on the day
after her husband suddenly dropped dead.
The rumour swept our street.  I didn't know
her well enough to call, or what to say.
The windows filled with dancing flakes.  It's said
that that way is the kindest way to go.
She's long lost touch, but I'm still here – that's how
I see her now, still looking at the snow.

# DISCARDED

This ring will go into the earth with her.
It's platinum, not gold, and very thin,
a token that I do not want to keep.
I sort her clothes, cast lipsticks in the bin,
recall how I was baffled as a child
by those inscriptions that said 'fell asleep'.

# DO NOT DISTURB

Some days I switch off telephones, the I-pad,
radio, the ubiquitous TV,
muffle the doorbell too, block out the jangling
voices of all who wish to get at me,

and ring you up, tell you (with lips just moving)
the family news.  Although the real phone's dead
and someone else has got your number, I can
still activate the line inside my head.

Another old friend gone.  And two more married.
The words are mouthed.  If you could hear, you'd know.
The baby was a girl.  No doubt, some people
would think me mad.  I tell you, even so.

# TORCHLIGHT

Now all the things they wished concealed
are spread before our eyes.
Embarrassment, too weak a word.
Exposed, the trivial lies.

We empty drawers, we send for scrap
the clothes in which they died.
The paper trail leads back to much
that they forgot to hide.

Pick up, ignite that feeble torch,
clutch Ariadne's thread
and cast a flickering light upon
the chambers of the dead.

# TRIPLETS
(North Hertfordshire Museum)

The first recorded set, but none
of these triplets saw the sun,
each a tiny skeleton.

Men extracted from the tomb
the third child, stuck still in her womb,

the second in her birth canal,
the first, between her thighs, but all

died.  See over this glass case
their mother's reconstructed face,

a flaxen-haired young woman, born
in Baldock, as it's now known.

Stranger, sigh and turn again,
count the bones, don't feel the pain,

go your way, and flip the page
on Britannia's Iron Age.

# AFTER HASTINGS

Some of Hastings has toppled into the sea.
This time, the giant rock killed no one, but
fast forward to another century
and people will abscond, their doors will shut,
the gracious Georgian terraces, the beach huts
be drowned, the crumbling castle overhead
collapse, the famous caves fill with salt water.
It might reach my old home, but I'll be dead,
the cliffs, like Robert Tressell's murals, gone,
and none look down on Hastings, except the moon.

# ON TUESDAY EVENINGS

On Tuesday evenings, I retreat into
my private, my most private office. There
they've placed a lamp, a glass and jug of water
(no stronger drink, my mind must not be clouded).
I hear doors closing, slowly all shuts down.
My civil servants shoot me looks of sympathy.

And then, when all are gone, I read the papers
again. Again I weigh the arguments,
my natural inclination to show mercy
against the need for lawful punishment.
The letters, tear-stained, badly spelled. The sordid
facts of the crime. The victim impact statements.

It's done. About a dozen times a year
I sign. An inexpressible relief.
Below me, in the street, the coloured lights
are flashing and the young are going crazy.
I snap my briefcase shut. I call my chauffeur.

Soon, they'll be gathering, a little crowd,
grey-faced, some on their knees, some mute, all counting.
The clock will strike. The hands move on. I'll sleep, though;
these cases always leave me drained. I know
someone has got to do this job. I hate it.

# ECLIPSE

Our shining faces, after prayers,
stared raptly at the Head.
'Today marks the eclipse, which I
shan't see again', he said.

'Yet you can surely hope, when you
have children of your own,
to see a second great event
in 1999'.

We peered through blackened bits of glass.
The tiny orange sun
revolved, re-kindled, blazed once more.
The Head died rather young.

And now my children walk into
the light, tread far from me,
remind me that the sun itself
one day will cease to be.

# CORONA DAYS

Corona days, trudging along the silent towpath
by the canal, wishing that it was the sea,
each day you hear, singing across the airwaves,
fresh news of death, divorce, disability.

How distant now the days when I was battling
three months ago, to set the world to rights!
Now, every trivial move must be considered.
I gasp for sea air.  I envy the red kites

that wheel above us, back from near-extinction,
enraptured, each day feasting on roadkill.
Celandines, crowsfoot fringe the path where few now
step out, spring colours, radiant and cruel.

*March 2020*

# ANTARCTICA

The penguins thought no harm.  They toddled up,
and clucked, and gazed at these strange bearded men.
The strangers were amused.
But it was necessary to kill the penguins.

This woman thought no harm.
She gladly let him come too close, but he
had wider aims, his core was cold.  He swung
his axe.  He left her bleeding on the ice.

# MARTHA'S WORLD

The world from space looked exquisite and perfect.
Men gasped at the extraordinary sight;
amazing skills it took to photograph it
in lovely hues, pure green, pure blue and white.
Yet something cautioned us, don't get too close,
don't see the dirty streams, the clouds of gas.

The child believed her man-made world was perfect
and blossomed in the six years since her birth,
played with a globe, identified the oceans;
two adults were the pillars of her earth,
until that day a weeping parent said
those words which made the world crash on her head.

# THIS PLACE

This place had a large shifting population –
a summer school, a holiday destination.
The parties went on far into the night.
They warned you, lock your door when you go out

even for a minute.  Men roamed around the campus
and it was no one's job to ask their business.
The couples lurched back underneath the moon
and laid their heads down in a rented room.

Yet that time, there was more to fear than theft.
A woman was attacked.  A child was left
deep sleeping, comfort blanket in her cot.
They warned them, lock your door, but some did not.

# HALLUCINATIONS

Once I saw, for a fraction of a second,
one who had gone, and once, I'm sure, I heard
his voice, tobacco-thickened but quite clear,
that said, 'No, Merryn, I am not here'.

I know that, know it was a hallucination
(though one child feared that I was going mad).
Though there exists no film, no voice recording –
too late – I'm confident of what I heard.

I cried out, 'So what did you mean by dying?
And don't you know what you have put us through?'
Again, there stretched the empty air between us;
whatever I had seen, it was not you.

# HOMAGE TO VERA MENCHIK

Washed up from Europe, speaking only Russian,
landed in Hastings, Vera, aged fifteen,
picked her laborious way across the pebbles
by that grey sea where I walked later on.

A round-faced teenager, living with her mother
and sister, English a pebble on her tongue -
but chess is a universal language, her absent
father said. Hastings Chess Club let her in.

Smiling rather than speaking, she caused amazement.
Men fell before her and were much annoyed.
They mocked but they were out-manoeuvred; several
reluctant males joined the Vera Menchik Club.

Hastings Castle looks down on figures that come and
go, and the endless movements of the sea.
None who played her are left; that board is empty,
kings, queens, black and white pawns all swept away.

Vera, her mother and her sister Olga
died together beneath a German bomb.
Her games were written down, and I can play them.
Vera Menchik, outstanding champion.

*Vera Menchik (1906–44)* was the undisputed Women's World Chess
Champion and one of the greatest woman players of all time. The Vera
Menchik Club was a name ironically proposed for the men she had beaten.

# VAVILOV
(Nikolai Ivanovich Vavilov, 1887–1943)

'Since you will almost certainly survive,
I ask you to remember that my name
is Vavilov, Academician.  My
ambition was to feed the world.  I gathered
seeds from each corner of the earth, and stored them',
he told the girl.  'Don't cry'.  They shuffled forward
in one long skein, across the dirty snow.
'I loved those seeds.  I wouldn't emigrate.
Swift said, he who can make two ears of corn
grow in a spot where only one grew previously
will do more good than all the politicians.
I thought, still think, no one need die of hunger',
he said.  Throughout the siege of Leningrad
his colleagues saved those seeds.  An asteroid,
a glacier, and a crater of the moon
are named for him.  He died at fifty-five,
emaciated.  The weeping girl survived.

# BOTTLE ALLEY

Bottle Alley was where I lounged in childhood,
within sounding distance of the sea,
walkway where a million glassy fragments
caught the changing light and winked at me.

Green or brown, more rarely red or yellow
(jewel-like vinaigrettes now ground to dust).
How I loved those glittering combinations –
chiefly purple, which meant Poisonous.

I am broken into little pieces.
2020 rolls towards its end,
one appalling year in which I suffered
smashed hopes, and the deaths of more than one friend.

Who now walks or skulks in Bottle Alley
where my schoolmates sheltered from the rain,
puffing fags or groping girls? I'll rally
slowly, fit myself together again.

# PORTRAIT OF A LADY IN HOVE ART GALLERY

Now the gallery is closed, because of Covid –
and it's in a depressing part of town –
my memory slowly travels back; I dream of
that picture, of a woman dressed in green.
She's in a small room full of books, extending
her hand, she can choose any from the shelf.
She has no name; the artist visualised her
quite young, but still liked being by herself.
The books will be her friends throughout the lockdown,
I don't think that she knew the Internet,
and when my library runs out, I look at –
in dreams – that picture which I can't forget.
Shielded from those drab streets, that stone-grey sea,
her quiet room is where I'd wish to be.

(Harold Knight, 'The Reader').

# THE KINGFISHER

The fourth time that I saw the kingfisher –
which unexpectedly streaked overhead,
or perched, precarious, on a swaying sapling –
and never realised that its breast was red –

at once depression lifted.  I am used to
infrequent sights of heron, grebe or owl,
yet hardly, in that bleak November, hoped for
this miracle.  Its flesh (they say) tastes foul,

but that does not concern me.  I can count them,
spaced out, those brief amazing times I've seen,
across my river, which moves all before it,
bears all away, that flash of brilliant green.

# HERMIONE

'How can it be imagined that Hermione, a virtuous and
affectionate wife, would conceal herself during sixteen years in a
solitary house, though she was sensible that her repentant
husband was all that time consuming away with grief and remorse
for her death?'
– Charlotte Lennox on *The Winter's Tale*, 1753.

He was angry, that I knew.
I could not tell what he might do.

His words raised firestorms in my head.
I let him think that I was dead.

Sixteen years I chose to spend
in hiding with a woman friend.

No let, the tears I bled and spilled
to mourn my children that he killed.

He had counselling, grew sane
and wished I was alive again.

'Step down, step down, Hermione;
he has suffered, hasn't he?

'Now he's normal and repents
sincerely, should you not relent?'

After all, my daughter lived.
That need not mean that I forgive.

# THE STRANGERS AT THE RESIDENTS' SUMMER PARTY

Some years ago, that family moved nextdoor,
a neighbour's guests, but only for the summer,
that time the Residents held their annual party.
I went; it was a lovely July evening.
Each household brought along some food and wine
to share, and urged the strangers to join in.
I fetched a Lego chest. Their little boy
chatted away in fluent Arabic
to me, enchanted by each coloured brick.
I answered him with gestures, smilingly.
Around us drifted adult conversations;
sun, chestnut shade, and his delight was obvious.
I thought of Syria, Palestine, Iraq,
and prayed, just keep him here, don't send him back.
Where next that family went, I wouldn't know;
the neighbour died, and others live there now.
From time to time, I do recall those visitors
(their names, if once we knew them, irretrievable),
and just today was jerked back to the past,
spotting a Lego fragment in the grass.

# AFTER CATULLUS

*'I don't look for your approval, Caesar, or care whether you are a black or a white man'.*

Why is that face all over social media?
Why must I contemplate it night and day?
I have no wish for your approval, Caesar,
nor interest in the vapid things you say.

Are you Stalin that I must keep staring,
fishlike, at your perfect suit and Brylcreemed hair?
Courtiers surround, another day they'll stab you;
include me out, for me you rank nowhere.

# THE GATEKEEPER

The floods in January swept away
that colony of swans. I counted hundreds
who nested by the Severn below Worcester
cathedral. It was 2020. Janus,
the two-faced god of endings and beginnings,
controlled that quiet month between disasters
past and to come, but I had no suspicion,
pacing the walkway in the winter sunshine.

Today the nests are drowned, the swans go flapping
about the streets like refugees, the dark
foul-smelling tide creeps upward. Other things
have happened, deaths, destruction of a marriage,
and lies in public life, and humans swallowed
beneath the Channel. Now the Janus gates
swing open. Where is it to end? we ask,
as that great weight of water tumbles through.

# AS YOU GET OLDER...

As you get older, letters start to trickle
through box or e-mail, food for tired eyes.
I knew the postcode, even knew the writing
when this one came; still, it was a surprise.

You had been ill, you said, had been reviewing
your life (how much of that is left?), which I
had briefly shared. Those names I hadn't thought of
for decades, aeons. A way to say goodbye?

# I SAW MY RIVAL

I saw her in an almost empty room,
years older now, and looking frail and sad,
her image bouncing back at me from Zoom
the dark disputed history we had had.
I looked, she also looked, we didn't speak.
So people fail, quite suddenly grow weak.

# IN CONVERSATION

Sorry to hear of your divorce.  But glad
it wasn't me you married.  Strange how news
filters through, long years afterwards, and I
kept quiet, never told the group I'd known you
better than they did.  We went back to talking
literature, someone mentioned Angel Clare,
and all laughed.  But I thought of that young woman
I never met, and of her children, and how
she panicked, and dropped gasping to the floor
half-conscious, when she saw you really meant it.

# REQUIEM FOR A WREN

After a while, the messages stopped coming,
that Covid winter, when the old and frail,
even if they could handle a PC,
did not get up, no longer wrote to me.
I used to get long letters, then came email;
after a while, though, clearly, she was too frail.
This Wren – the last? – outlived her generation,
husband, child, friends. The messages stopped coming.

# RED WHITE AND BLUE

When I drive past an elder in full flower
on June roads, on some national holiday,
I yearn for its distinctive scent and colour.
There was a poet who saw cow parsley

not as a weed, but a luxuriant
drift of pure colour, white as you need to get.
The wayside is alive; red is a field of
poppies, and blue is vivid alkanet.

Tatty bunting obscures the war memorial,
and through the road signs, grass has overgrown.
I look elsewhere – these flags do not concern me –
prefer frail flora and enduring stone.

# TO RUTH
(Ruth Bidgood, 1922– 2022)

You told me how, in 1941, you
walked with your boyfriend quietly through Port Meadow
not far from Thames, and watched the nesting moorhens,
not talking much, not asking what came next.
You vowed you'd write, you did exchange long letters,
and he survived, but married someone else.

And now it's 2022, and war
again, not that it ever stopped, or will.
I see them, lovers clinging to each other
in tears, before just one gets on the train –
the young men not allowed to cross the border –
and time winds back, the scene is just the same.
Two students walk, him with his call-up papers,
and you a girl the age of Sophie Scholl,
across a field of memory, and it darkens,
and I'll remember, though your light grows frail.

# ELEGY
(for Ruth Bidgood)

I learned of your death in a crowded seafront café
between trains, flicking casually through my smartphone
as everyone does.  I should have expected this news
but didn't.  You'd not have felt at home in this place,

distrusting the sea, turning back to the mountains. So
I went for a last look, and spent a half hour counting
the waves, remembering how I'd watched them crashing
off Hengistbury Head, on the actual day you died.